LEARN
TOGETHER

READING AND WRITING 3
Capital letters, rhyming words

Sandra Soper

MACMILLAN
CHILDREN'S BOOKS

Note to parents

The aim of this book is to encourage your child to read and write at home. Young children love to copy. If you read and write with pleasure and purpose, your child will want to copy you. Also, the enthusiasm you show for the work in this book will rub off on the child. The activities are designed to be interesting and enjoyable: young children absorb more when they are happy and interested. Concentration varies from child to child, but 10 to 20 minutes per session is a good guide. Watch out for signs of weariness and stop before the work becomes boring.

In this series we use flicked letters from the very beginning to make it easier for the child to progress to fully joined-up writing. This has long been seen as good practice and is now recommended by the National Curriculum. Your child's school will have an agreed handwriting style. Find out what it is and use it whenever you write out something for the child to copy so that you complement the work of the school. It will hinder your child's progress if there is a conflict of advice between home and school.

Read the verses aloud, then copy them.

A was an aeroplane
some folk say 'plane.

B was a buffalo
roaming the plain.

C was a cowboy
who branded a cow.

D was a dinosaur
they're extinct now.

Colour the pictures which go with the verses above.

Which sound is in the middle? Join each word to its middle sound then write the word again.

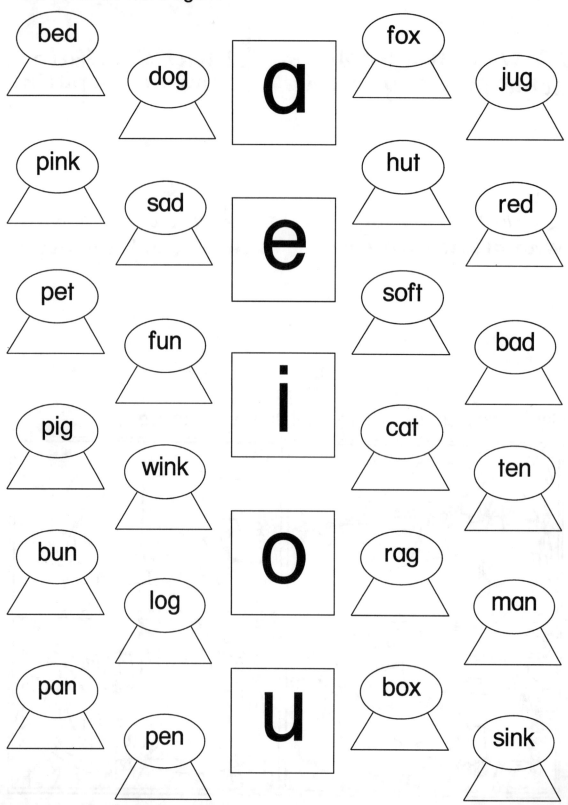

bed

dog

fox

jug

a

pink

sad

hut

red

e

pet

fun

soft

bad

i

pig

wink

cat

ten

bun

log

rag

man

o

pan

pen

box

sink

u

Copy the verse in your best handwriting and colour the border in blue and green.

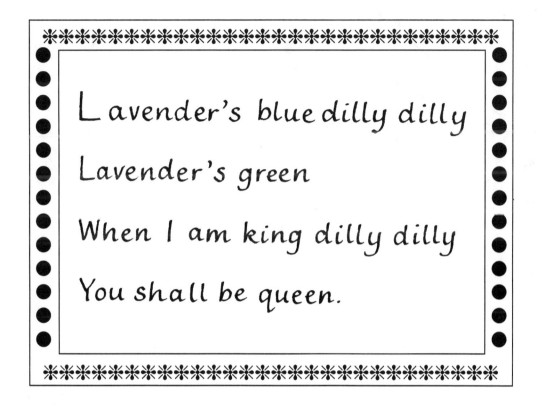

Lavender's blue dilly dilly

Lavender's green

When I am king dilly dilly

You shall be queen.

Sound each 'sh' word then write it in the box.

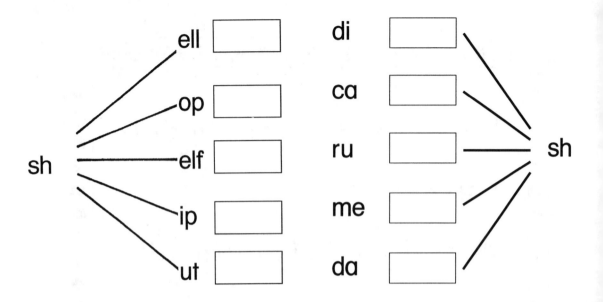

ell [ ]   di [ ]

op [ ]   ca [ ]

sh   elf [ ]   ru [ ]   sh

ip [ ]   me [ ]

ut [ ]   da [ ]

Can you fill the shell with 'sh' words?

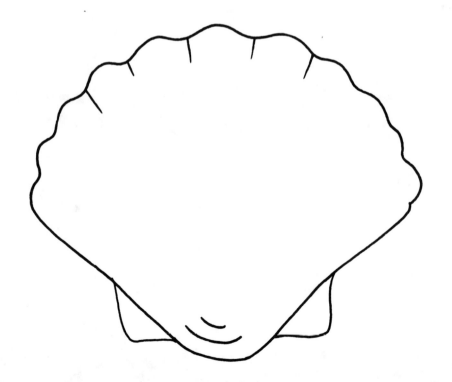

Write an 'i' in each square, then sound the letters along to make one word and down to make another word.

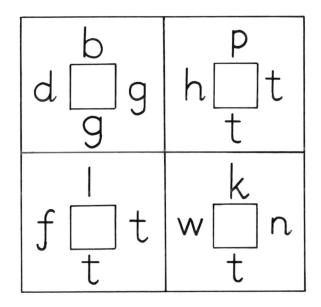

1 _dig_
2 _big_
3 _____
4 _____
5 _____
6 _____
7 _____
8 _____

Read these sentences and underline the words from the puzzle above. Can you make up some more sentences using these words?

A bird uses its beak to dig for worms.

The big bad wolf tried to trick Red Riding Hood.

Cinderella's glass slipper did not fit the ugly sisters' feet.

When the hare raced the tortoise the hare did not win.

Go over the capital letters in felt pen, then read the alphabet aloud.

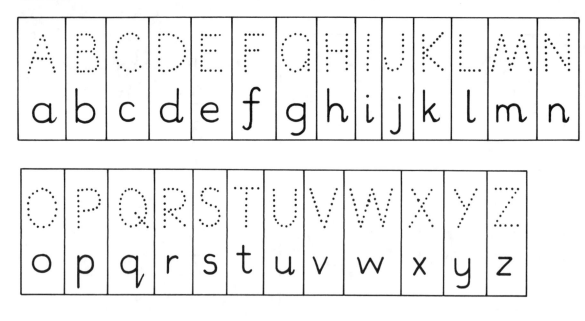

Read then colour the words.

Read the verses aloud, then copy them out in large writing.

E was an eagle
with very wide wings

F was a goldfish
with very fine fins.

G was a gardener
who grew lovely flowers

H was a harpist
who practised for hours

Colour the pictures which go with the verses above.

Can you help McBean to sound the words then write them?

ba — d _____
   — g _____
   — t _____

ma — d _____
   — n _____
   — t _____

ha — m _____
   — s _____
   — d _____

da — d _____
   — m _____
   — b _____

ca — t _____
   — n _____
   — p _____

ra — t _____
   — n _____
   — g _____

fi — g _____
   — n _____
   — t _____

pi — t _____
   — n _____
   — g _____

Go over the capitals, then read the lines aloud.

A is for apple,

B is for ball,

C is for cuddle,

D is for doll,

E is for empty,

F is for fill,

G is for garden,

H is for hill.

Read the words, then join the capital to the same small letter.

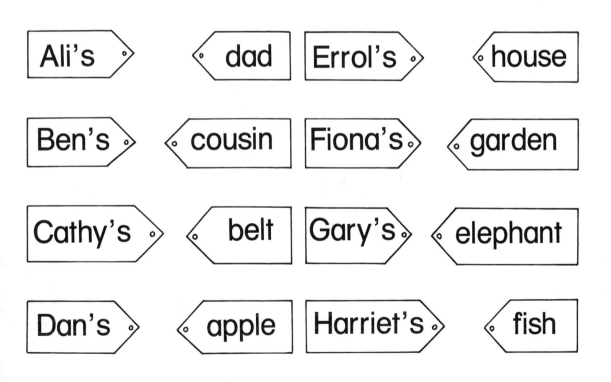

Ali's — dad | Errol's — house

Ben's — cousin | Fiona's — garden

Cathy's — belt | Gary's — elephant

Dan's — apple | Harriet's — fish

What am I? Write the answers in sentences.

I shine at night and start with 's.'

I have four wheels and start with 'c.'

I give you milk and start with 'c.'

I can bounce and start with 'b.'

Colour the pictures, then label them.

Read each word, then join it to its middle sound and write the
word underneath.

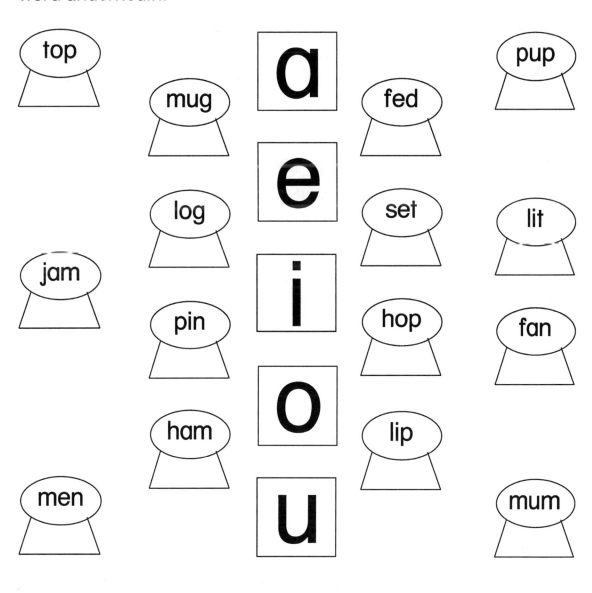

top   mug   a   fed   pup

log   e   set   lit

jam

pin   i   hop   fan

ham   o   lip

men   u   mum

Can you underline the word above which comes into this
proverb?

See a pin and pick it up,
All the day you'll have good luck.

Can you help McBean to sound the words then write them?

be < d ———   pe < t ———   ru < g ———
       g ———   n ———   n ———

le < g ———   ro < t ———
       t ———   d ———

fe < n ———   me < n ———   lo < t ———
       d ———   t ———   g ———

Underline the words above which come into these proverbs. Do you know what they mean?

Early to bed, early to rise
Makes us all healthy wealthy and wise.

You shouldn't try to run
before you can walk.

Spare the rod
and spoil the child.

14

Read the verses aloud, then copy them out in clear handwriting.

I was an imp
who couldn't sit still.

J was the Jack
who fell down the hill.

K was King Cole
a merry old soul.

L was the lass
who scored the first goal.

Colour the pictures to go with the verses above.

Go over the capital letters, then read the lines aloud.

I is for in,

J is for jump,

K is for king,

L is for lump,

M is for milk,

N is for not,

O is for orange,

P is for pot.

Read the words, then join the capital to the same small letter.

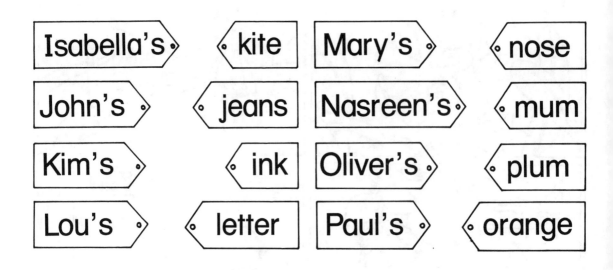

Isabella's	kite	Mary's	nose
John's	jeans	Nasreen's	mum
Kim's	ink	Oliver's	plum
Lou's	letter	Paul's	orange

Write an 'a' in each square, then sound the letters along to make one word and down to make another word.

```
 b        c
b □ g   c □ t
 d        n

 D        j
d □ b   j □ b
 n        m
```

1 _bad_
2 _bag_
3 _____
4 _____
5 _____
6 _____
7 _____
8 _____

Read the sentences and underline the words from the puzzle above.

The tree was blown down in the bad storm.

I carry books to school in a plastic bag.

McBean can dance and sing. Can you?

My cat is black and is called liquorice.

What am I? Can you write the answers to the questions in sentences?

I start with 'h' and you wear me on your head.

I end with 'll' and you can ring me.

I rhyme with tall and you can bounce me.

I start and end with 'b' and babies wear me.

Colour then label the pictures.

Read the verses aloud, then copy them out.

M was a muffin
sold by a man.

N was a noodle
cooked in a pan.

O was an orange
which looked good to eat.

P was a pig
with trotters for feet.

Colour the pictures to go with the verses above.

Go over the capital letters, then read the verses aloud.

Q is for queen,

R is for rhyme,

S is for sand,

T is for time,

U is for under,

V is for vest,

W is for wool,

can you say the rest?

X   Y   Z

Read the words, then join each capital to the same small letter.

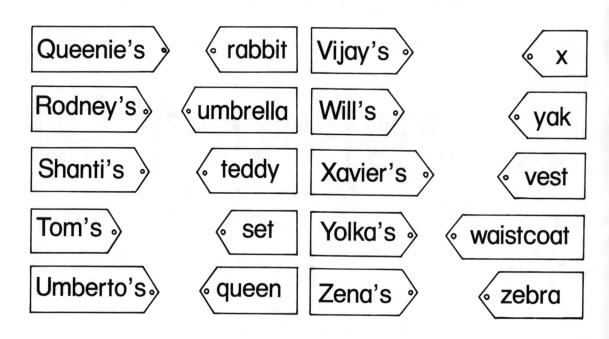

Queenie's — rabbit   Vijay's — x

Rodney's — umbrella   Will's — yak

Shanti's — teddy   Xavier's — vest

Tom's — set   Yolka's — waistcoat

Umberto's — queen   Zena's — zebra

Read the rhyme aloud.

Old Mother Hubbard

Went to the cupboard

To fetch her poor dog a bone,

But when she got there

The cupboard was bare

And so the poor dog had none.

Go over the words, then join those which rhyme. You can go over rhyming words in the same colour.

Mother

Hubbard

done

there

bare

cupboard

brother

What can you find in the cupboard? Match the labels then colour them. Ring the labels which you cannot find. Draw some more labels if you can.

CUSTARD

HONEY

TEA BAGS

PEANUT BUTTER

INSTANT COFFEE

FLOUR

COCOA

MARMITE

Sound the 'th' words, then write them in the box.

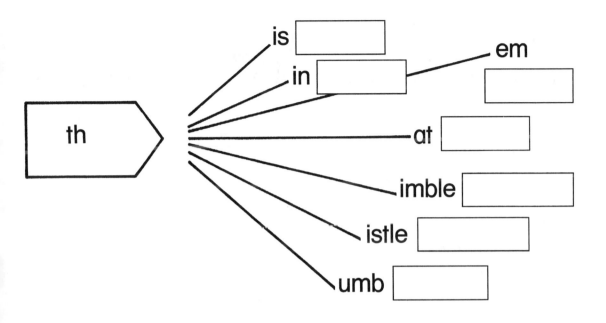

th
is ☐
in ☐
em
☐
at ☐
imble ☐
istle ☐
umb ☐

Can you fill the thistle with 'th' words?

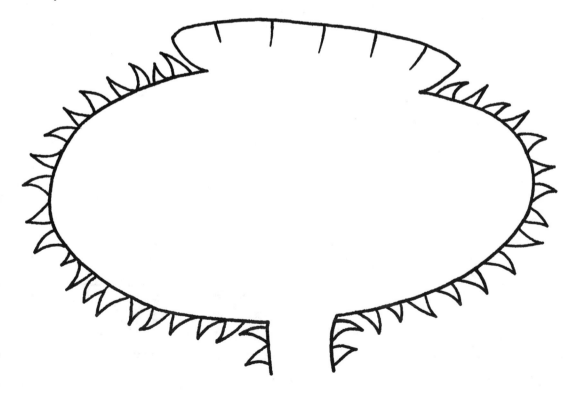

Read the verses aloud, then copy them out in your best handwriting.

Q was a queen
singing sweetly in tune.

R was a rocket
which zoomed to the moon.

S was a swallow
high in the sky.

T was a tortoise
clambering by.

Colour the pictures to go with the verses above.

Can you sound these words which start with 'ch' and write them in the boxes?

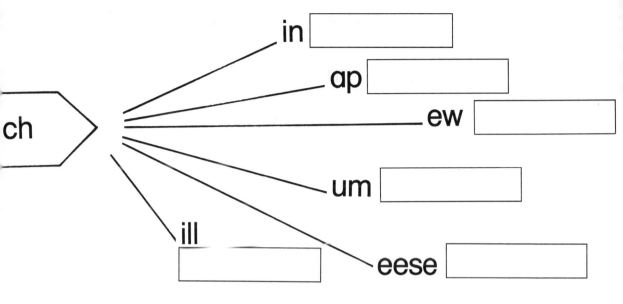

ch

in ☐

ap ☐

ew ☐

um ☐

ill ☐

eese ☐

Write 'ch' at the end of these letters to make a word. Sound the word, then write the whole word in the empty box.

mu	
su	
hut	
wit	
fet	
mat	

Read more verses of Old Mother Hubbard.

She went to the tailor's
To buy him a coat,
But when she came back
He was riding a goat.

She went to the hatter's
To buy him a hat,
But when she came back
He was feeding the cat.

Go over the words, then read them aloud. Use felt pens to go over the rhyming words in the same colour, then join them with that colour.

tailor
coat
hatter
hat

goat
sailor
cat
matter

Read the verses aloud, then colour the pictures.

U was an uncle
who went off to sea.

V was a vest
which didn't fit me.

W was a wizard
who cast spells for fun.

X is the cross
you put on the bun.

Y is for 'yippee'
I yelled when I heard

that Z's the last letter
which has to be learned.

Z A B C D E F G H
I J K L M N O P Q R S
T U V W X Y Z

Practise your capitals.

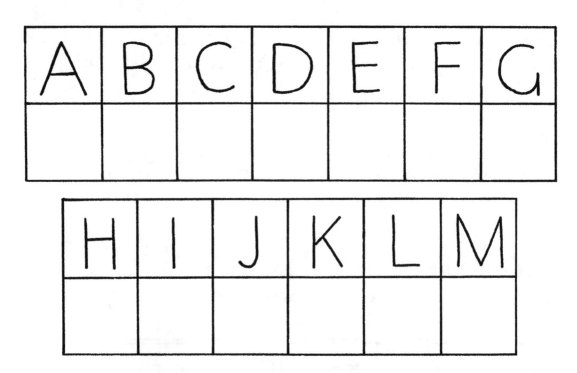

Can you write these names again in capital letters?

Lulu	Billy	Bianca

Nasmin	Deon	David

Sound the 'wh' words, then write them in the boxes.

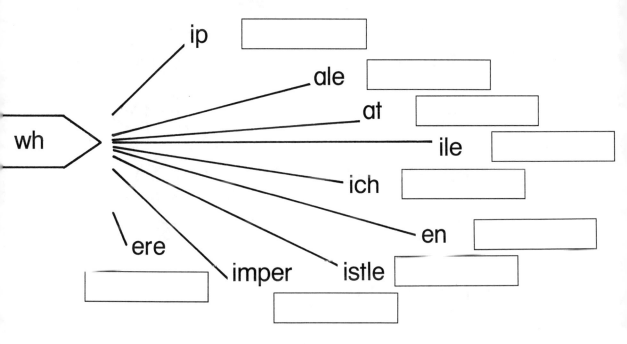

wh

ip
ale
at
ile
ich
en
istle
imper
ere

Decorate the whale with 'wh' words.

Read the rhyme aloud.

Little Jack Horner

Sat in a corner

Eating a Christmas pie.

He put in his thumb

And pulled out a plum

And said, "What a good boy am I."

Can you fill the pie with food words?

What am I and what colour am I? Write the answers in sentences.

You can post your letters into me.

Cows like to eat me.

You can make a snowman with me.

I am the same colour as my name and good to eat.

Colour and label the pictures.

Practise your capitals.

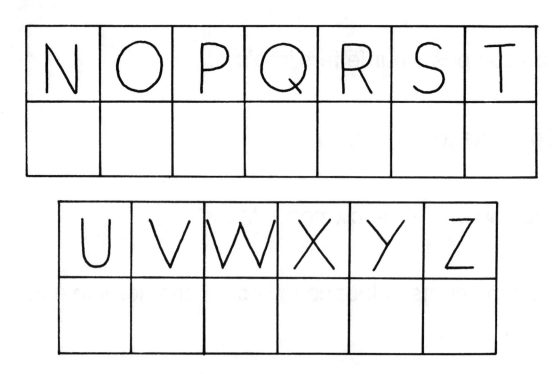

Re-write these names using only capital letters.

Hassan	Bob	Catherine

William	Sara	Vincent